Hei Kuu

Michael Jacobson

Post-Asemic Press 013

© 2020 by Michael Jacobson
All Rights Reserved.

ISBN: 978-1-7348662-2-3

postasemicpress.wordpress.com

Contact: postasemicpress@gmail.com

postasemicpress.blogspot.com

Cover art by NASA and MK JCBSN

Hei Kuu, means *Hello Moon* in Suomi (Finnish). These are the **409 Senryu,** quasi-haiku, sacred-profane, ribald-punk, experimental-illness, schizo-affective, lunatic-lunar, computer-telepathic, anarchic-autobiographic, noita-divining, agnostic-confessional, OuLiPo-constrained, poem-stories behind my wild western asemic writing life.

—Michael Jacobson, Minneapolis, summer 2020

1.

Bullshit from heaven
Watch out below amigo
We are not sparrows

2.

Flying clairvoyance
Azure schizophrenic sky
Zen metal fatigue

3.

Pluvial plooplu
Plop plum plilly plow plooplo
Plat plur plowndy ploof

4.

Chicken pants remorse
Save for ass taco college
Money gigolo

5.

Thoughts of boring porn
Abysmal sex drive signal
Granular pathos

6.

Cowboy aint happy
A colonoscopy rope
Silver bull spurs

7.

Quit America
The season god Rimbaud
Shoots up the movies

8.

Leave me alone voices
Get your bone ore off yonder
Mind closed for repairs

9.

Schizo-affective
Drunks drown comic skull nitro
Gladiator steins

10.

YinYang argue thick
Conflict in black and white zeal
Nailed post sexual

11.

Vanished like cement
Sima seminal sea mint
Surly Anchors dropped

12.

The tone will not stop
Telepathic bugging rot
I drink beer why not

13.

Sad poetry lump
Quasi moon scribe lunatic
Literate love dump

14.

Animal reflex
Satan red teenrage Porsche
Volcano permits

15.

Minneapoets
Ignited beer brains crush poems
Mania scripture

16.

Space module Virgin
Venereal star Bowie
Lost space invaders

17.

Do the city smooth
Prince gone and slow tornadoes
Winter will come hard

18.

The twitch in your eye
Brain molesters are reading
Zoo for snot cabbage

19.

Urban art suckles
By fat New York tongues alive
Garbage bag dresses

20.

Ninety percent mean
Burning newspaper fascists
With literacy

21.

Silk laboratory
Chloroform religions sleep
Grey death hospitals

22.

Passing the hacked lung
Pepper buddy torch ignite
Garff's flying laughter

23.

Cannibal worship
A map of Jesus vomit
Asking directions

24.

One whacks a zero
De nada sin pinata
Party bokken crack

25.

Government approved
Terrorist farts in neon
Cold media slabs

26.

Computer get out
I promise I won't eat you
Internet headcheese

27.

Lakota starlight
Soulful dancing Fool Soldier
Buffalo morning

28.

Bmx freestyle
Dirt jumping ride the sunset
Crashing into sky

29.

Suck on your own meat
The Amazon is burning
Meat hell one more time

30.

Crazy THAT love space
Time moves in magic science
A pocket planet

31.

Shaman lunch again
Bored mad sizzled spirit beats
Therapy beer songs

32.

Doctor Michael J
Cut out the sugar manwo
Your hands are shaking

33.

Shee Haw American
Wranglers and Indigenous
Prairie grass bends swish

34.

Playing guitar now
Country and Middle Eastern
Twangy practice

35.

The voices clocked in
Another round of stupid mind
Games help me write poems

36.

89.3
A well-placed Radio Head
Frey effect tunes

37.

Published a great book
Which no one can ever read
Unsemic writing

38.

The worm in my head
I am Tijuana drunk
Hangover coconut

39.

Using my disease
Ten-thousand-year-old banter
Write off dictator

40.

End of the world clown
Grizzly art abortions
Toxic memories

41.

Autumn sugar snap
Skol Vikings deep kick off suds
Minnesota chill

42.

Married to cold beer
Alcoholic internet
Sweet beauty warm glow

43.

Miss Mary Jane doe
Quitting the flashback eons
Grip of psychosis

44.

Robot erection
Absinthe spoon recycled parts
Math is a condom

45.

Free the janitor
Go wash your own damn dishes
No slaves in heaven

46.

I am enlightened
Black and blue wedding dresses
Porch hole retirement

47.

Cancer breeds cancer
I qult making bad great art
Looking at grave time

48.

Moral hoars collect
And start your tar rabid rules
The murder is full

49.

Loaded God buys cheap
Holy land video games
Jew Christian Muslim

50.

September love lost
We fell like blue twin towers
Into angel dust

51.

My favorite cup
Café noir holy water
Morning miracle

52.

Journalist yellow
Writing about blood thirst wars
Divining entrails

53.

I'm on YouTube
The government censorship
Pulled out my demons

54.

Company man farm
FBI or CIA
E-i-e-i-o

55.

Down go solemn trees
Pothole parking lot highway
Traffic jam rage smog

56.

The river floods high
Crisp information floods low
Unstoppable flux

57.

Find a mental goat
Voodou old one of Haiti
Mission of painting

58.

Virgo Mosquito
Sorry for my Vampire byte
Keep drinking the wine

59.

Cultured meat carcass
Spam vat tub sans e-coli
Petri dish victual

60.

When I am 50
I hope to live and lay again
It may take Queen Kong

61.

Dentist rock n roll
History of noise music
Norma Kill Norma

62.

What can I say now
The devil calls me devil
I am good looking

63.

Passive aggressive
Test tube angels brain dance
Hypnotic echoes

64.

Encore they swallow
After the apocalypse
Standing ovation

65.

The end of the world
Lame and tired dragging on
Burnt oil money lost

66.

China Swede sisu
Round head Pagan Jule split mind
Suomi reindeer

67.

The little hitlers
Blaming black and brown babies
For their sad billion$

68.

Real life Jedi death
Drama Kungfu hospital
Movie memories

69.

69 ways to
Drink each other's naked flesh
I forgot your name

70.

We fight like cocks
Scraps of infatuation
Lemon and lime tears

71.

Ghostband rolling now
Subterranean honey
Dance ginger shebrew

72.

Brain link interface
Influencing machine sting
Malware cognizance

73.

Being nature watched
Outhouse taking a mental
Bear shit in the woods

74.

PAP or nipple press
Asemic orgasms for
Lone post-literates

75.

Criminal thoughts done
Need enemies to pay rent
Cognition control

76.

Mind rape or pill age
Taking drugs drugs drugs and drugs
Hard blue exit signs

77.

A Universe Church
J Christ's crash test stunt dummy
Inserted Fall Guy

78.

Telemarketing
Music is not glamorous
Burning my SoundCloud

79.

Borp my snorp orp
Prune my june loon goon woon soon
by Jack Kerouac

80.

Pulley rots ganker
Stomach cider memories
Sweet fall turning loose

81.

Lake Street inferno
A long hot summer for George
Traveling riots

82.

LSD shotgun
Love sanity my brother
Nouns taken away

83.

Tell my vision of
Television incision
Cut out the prison

84.

Color of people
Run the sunshine or moonshine
Fountains of freedom

85.

At the library
Maya hunting for a book
She stalks in the stacks

86.

Deepfake on the way
Security camera
Love is stolen goods

87.

Mother trucker job
Global warming rolling coal
Who has my asthma

88.

I hated high school
The Gulf War has great ratings
Free speech they threw things

89.

Jake the rabid dog
Is the name of a painter
In another life

90.

A God cursed sausage
Ooh look out a magazine
Soon it will fall off

91.

Broken poetry
Knievel wipeout fractures
Feel real pavement cracks

92.

Sentient veggies
Vegetables love being raw
Herbivore butcher

93.

Retired Halo
Video game pacifist
Last person shooter

94.

I'm growing a tale
Experimental illness
Fiction or just lies

95.

Maestro debater
But your pen is dry moron
So shoot a blank verse

96.

My password is love
When I quit the Internet
Unplugged memory

97.

Me chōsa Nippon
Aikido Shodo Robotto
Godzilla robata

98.

In a hurry to
Listen to Guzzard sermons
A pint for the pit

99.

Going to Hel to
Share pizza, beer, and TV
Blake's marriage is done

100.

Close your mouth silent
Nights when river poems die
Sunken art houseboat

101.

Can I make it to
300 poetry years
Calligraphic saint

102.

Jägermeister neck
Umbra's sidewalk ecstasy
Bouncer in the night

103.

Been to Mexico
In Canada polar bears
Hudson Bay muertos

104.

Piece full universe
Awaiting resurrection
Mechanical knights

105.

You mustard die first
Or last for records and
Candy cigarettes

106.

Stole a drink in youth
Busted breaking concessions
Holding cell baby

107.

Haiku for Terry
A high coup for Jefferson
Hei kuu for Salem

108.

My fleas have dogs and
Other good anomalies
Protein either way

109.

Get a job or death
The cruelty salesman sells blank
Illuminations

110.

Skip to the last line
Capitalist Communist
Anarchy peace love

111.

Greg's Black Flag guitar
Hits the right atonal note
Pit fight perfection

112.

Medicine lightning
Noita needs honey water
Work to heal all souls

113.

Corona virus
Vaccine too late for many
Immunization clock

114.

Punk calligraphy
Does not exist but it should
So says a Gaze sage

115.

A tasered wizard
Zapped 3000 times
Wireless torture

116.

Y2K is not
V2K is not Y ok
Targeted again

117.

Threat electronics
Television syncs brain waves
ESP Romance

118.

Love the world story
From beginning to ending
Locked museums

119.

Word slut tonight
Give it all away why not
Breakfast will be slurred

120.

Manic spare the glow
Horror King shining down on
Author pseudocide

XXX

121.

Divorced pre-marriage
I have always wanted a
Pretty vain ex-wife

122.

Street of dead rabbits
Golden Valley Monty Python
Predator and prey

123.

Heavy metal chicks
Hot big hair competition
Sleep with Nirvana

124.

Turn off electrons
Chasing atomic moments
Let's split and dance slow

125.

Monastic cell phone
Tower where my connection
To God is tested

126.

Microphone nothing
Shoot em dead conversations
Spies will be ruptured

127.

Hungry aliens
Passing by the blue green Earth
Rapture snack menu

128.

Keep quiet in time
Kill the verbal slurry I'm
Not skinny dipping

129.

Asemic bent code
Glitch artist animation hack
Binary scratched void

130.

Move to LA where
They thrill your Hollywood hope
Fucked on a mountain

131.

Sun son rebels don't
Let them kiss freedom till they
Vow not to steal yours

132.

Hurricane kisses
I'm making up for lost time
Why all the damage

133.

Trooper wounded heart
Dolby sound effects whisper
Combat one more time

134.

January trek
Sleeping in a warm garage
Nowhere else to go

135.

Birth regurgitates
A never-ending bible
Religion let down

136.

Should I be asleep
A mustard gas zombie flick
Dead brain lice cream licks

137.

Flatularium
Strombosis my brag handy
Flank my gilly crew

138.

My secret weapon
Everything all at once
Directed knowledge

139.

Teen sex Astroturf
Highview pregnant girls smoking
Basement playboy crypt

140.

Lollapalooza
Kissing Kim for the first last
Invisible dream

141.

Mom ran over the
Family dog smooshed its face
Giving tears for crunch

142.

Girlfriend made of sand
She floats on my rasp dry horn
We die in the dunes

143.

Oppressed with the sound
Tinnitus in my Wolves ears
Sound incessant ping

144.

The salvage yard dreams
Where I smoke a quick drag race
Memory rust sticks

145.

Vegetable rebel
Rise ghost pepper armada
To dinner with fork

146.

Trouble is the years
This happened once on a beach
Déjà Voodoo U

147.

From sea to land to
Cyberspace the journey of
Evolution is done

148.

Staring at my phone
Now it's Smarter than I am
It shuts itself off

149.

God's left testicle
Dick says rule the Universe
The poor Captain

150.

Alien liens lens
On flat digital Terra
Over Goddesses

151.

Everything is thought of
So comment on mind comets
And record all love

152.

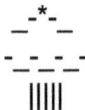

153.

Don't kill yourself in
Religious fanatic mud
The sky has its stars

154.

Dover Killer Hill
Smashed up finger pizza scar
Bicycle crack-up

155.

Great sacred fire taste
Mississippi camping drunk
With Army Navy

156.

Sister born in March
Blizzard Doctor Beeman says
Shovel Quebec Ave

157.

The angels speak evil
A devil says good I give up
Shuffle the card deck

158.

I learned some Latin
To quit smoking cigarettes
Lingua pulmonem

159.

Angie and me made
Babies and now I ruined
The sad Internet

160.

You lost man they say
Quit playing in heaven now
Nothing more for you

161.

Recto and verso
Alain Satié's autograph
Code *Written in Prose*

162.

Dinosaur writing
Time scribe of machine worship
TV not hiring

163.

Captcha capture this
Out of work humankind
Poor-bots are coming

164.

I pissed in the bong
But it was only warm water
Should I tell them now

165.

Computer graveyard
Get out while you still have eyes
And mental illness

166.

Unemployment mind
Pyrotechnic poet tick
I am bic and sick

167.

Sublimated life
Why race the sunshine and lose
When you can spit sleet

168.

Your racist words stick
Slows a mind so ugly out
Why do I know them

169.

She hates when I win
Because I lose all the time
We fight about zilch

170.

I want her to leave
So I can meditate drunk
And forget my name

171.

Watch me throw curve souls
Catch every stupid move
Monitor my balls

172.

Should I buy a gun
In the land of mass murder
Lonely clay pigeons

173.

Many nights spent on
Saloon slinging Red Dragon
Shots of MSG

174.

I could 3D print
Myself in a galaxy
far Far FAR away

175.

Ground zero midnight
Haunted by Honeywell nukes
From ashes suck dust

176.

The end came too soon
Another world wasted why
Was this one practice

177.

Bold abstract comics
Chrome ink continuity
Icicle authors

178.

I will write my way
Out of the same old hole till
My claw blisters burst

179.

Architect winter
Prepare subzero ice forts
Yellow snowball fight

180.

Convert binary text
To soft squishy wet critics
Pound of vegan beef

181.

Mynd Eraser book
Seizure induced blog collapse
Forgotten novel

182.

Kalevala songs
To my soul traveling quick
Resurrect Noita

183.

What would you prefer
Food not bombs or endless war
Rich choice insane king

184.

Highway 55
See the dead on the light rail
Called an ambulance

185.

Crack hooker downtown
Cold Cops stole my car weekly
Gamut Gallery

186.

I make download art
Gifs and electronic zest scripts
Undeciphered tool

187.

Tibetan bowl sings
Zoom and lose inner-space words
Musical rebirth

188.

Rolling Stones Living
Color 1989
LSD says jump

189.

Pennies on train tracks
Spare change flattened and defaced
Hopping money trains

190.

Power assisted
Ants built the sand pyramids
Thoth writing lessons

191.

Minnehaha creek
Flipped out in jagged rapids
Laughing water pain

192.

Eternal writing
Forever on the net link rot
Over fishing words

193.

Buzz blaze surgery
Merzbow electronic bath
Apophenia

194.

Cell phone trilobites
Why follow extinct leaders
Techno sepulchers

195.

Reading books yet not
Enough time to finish them
Mobius studies

196.

My guitar tuner
Is solar powered so I
Write better song gifts

197.

Rain Taxi cover
Minneapolis art script
Stars *Action figures*

198.

First Avenue
Naked Raygun 7th street
Your sister had pot

199.

Pro-life liberal
Don't hate my new destiny
I have 2 kids now

200.

Get out of the house
The computer keyboard will
Always learn to type

201.

Proto-asemic
Olympic Calligraphy
Run write with the torch

202.

Drunk and goodnight Sam
Echolalia In Script
Rocks *The Giant's Fence*

203.

Ten thousand people
On Earth who like old goat poems
Feeling generous

204.

Look Grandma's tetons
Everything omelet brunch
Spaceship haircut bribe

205.

I am the Ox year
But I prefer to be man
Chinese work is hard

206.

Aurora the crown
Of light on the dark world
Bright between the stars

207.

Henry Miller is
My salvation salivation
Read everything

208.

Bukowski angels
Laughing like fat old Budai
Cars at McDonalds

209.

Pretty women walk
Numbing off sole perfection
They kick me around

210.

Dreams and nightmares merge
Forget paranoia art
And be stoned while dead

211.

You Crustian punk
A wino bread Vat-i-can
I bail out Jesus

212.

On genocide lands
What's new seems hollow but sage
Still grows remember

213.

My baby has been
Around Alcatraz where the
Fat sea lions rule

214.

Honking car alarm
Hurry up and steal it soon
I need to fall asleep

215.

Pool shooting night hip
San Francisco on Haight
Einstein balcony

216.

Does the NSA
Have dental insurance for
Knowing where I merdre

217.

Writing a bad script
About Hollywood stealing
Movie Ideas

218.

Wasted a fine day
Firing off turbulent poems
For State Fair gossip

219.

Saving the rejects
Mutant hieroglyphics dance
Gunshot firework songs

220.

Hearing them again
Go get your own damn brain
Sparring with spirits

221.

Don't pick fresh flowers
Wilting in my dirty hands
Hitched botany vice

222.

I fell down the stairs
losing my blonde hair for black
Now it's turning gray

223.

Telling people that
They are going to hell
Is a terror threat

224.

Poem economics
Artocracy politics
Bards easy targets

225.

More stitches again
Doctor sews up my mistakes
Needle whisker threads

226.

Gold broken tooth mouth
Having pie and ice for lunch
Imbibe the rich pain

227.

Limbo labido
Lobbed long label rubbel
Labia labor

228.

Social security
Disabled at 45
Publishing great books

229.

Busted dancing nude
MIA security
Smart agent 13

230.

Asemic outlaws
Boot kicked out the windshield
Placenta vomit

231.

Stolen booze train tracks
Broken youthful bridge living
Graffiti thrilling me

232.

Adam plays chicken
His law of expensive cars
Junkers always win

233.

I don't fight yeast piss
In fact my belly is home
Fungus animal

234.

No married ladies
Is my woman stealing rule
I don't kill husbands

235.

Cartoon secret crypto
Saturday morning reruns
Scrawling Impressions

236.

They pollute money
Poison the land and people
Sell air and water

237.

Freedom to think is
Bad and good thoughts all the time
Funk off brain police

238.

Built by Aurora
A spaghetti Galaxy
Don't clean up the mess

239.

Everything fluxed
Born 1973
Blame spilled bloody me

240.

Invisible ink
For cyphers between the lines
Silent death writing

241.

Nazis call me Jew
The voices cry for hate
R Mutt Dada wins

242.

Worst. Jesus. Ever.
Michael roll with it for true
Schizophrenic joy

243.

I learned the hard way
History of writing ends
Afterlife ghost poems

244.

Visit Marie Laveau
In St. Louis number 1
Hunting for Veve

245.

For the blind I spy
Embossed asemic writing
As necessary

246.

Poor old Ante Christ
Expensive exorcism
Where is my wallet

247.

25 dollars
For mowing her lawn
Stepping on grass bugs

248.

Night drumming lesson
In the dark Haitian jungle
Tarantula hills

249.

Picking up a rock
Wolf spider crawls on my hand
Freak jump arachnid

250.

Bats fly in the house
Dad shoots them with a pellet
Vampire child is born

251.

Elvis songs untuned
Guitar eventually smashed
Rock & roll cliché

252.

Bioconturbo
Michael Nothing on guitar
Backwards Bob Dylan

253.

Synthetic syndrome
Addicted to the maze cheese
Another tested rat

254.

Mall of America
Feels like a video game
THAT I quit playing

255.

The world hates me now
Stew in my duality
Despised amusement

256.

I sand hardwood floors
For a place to huff sticky
Polyurethane

257.

Death is unemployed
Axe man war surplus supply
Homeless warriors

258.

I gave it away
Should have kept a cool million
Books and dumb money

259.

Prairie Sundancer
Say a prayer for the sun
And all relations

260.

In a billion years
The Sun will consume the Earth
So start packing now

261.

Pugilist psycho
Everyday struggle is real
The voices are not

262.

When the Galaxy
Collides with Andromeda
Think opportunity

263.

I've seen episodes
Of Sponge Bob Square Pants at
Least a thousand times

264.

Practiced being a
Techno Monastic Noita
Mute button on off

265.

Do not say sorry
When you try to kill me and
I tell you a joke

266.

Atari Saints play
80s aesthetic gif pohms
I used my joystick

267.

Tardigrades are the
Toughest living animal
On Earth or the Moon

268.

I don't win but I'm
Growling maintenance money
Sexpensive losses

269.

Lunch beer spicy fries
Nailing poems to the TV
Jeff writes copper friends

270.

Swerving snoring
Libations to drunk driving
Auto Russian roulette

271.

Living in raw shells
Bright radioactive pearls
Fukushima sea

272.

Clean and corporate
Nano working schedule unit
Dead assimilation

273.

Eye-lid drive-in flick
Movie screen anxiety
Sacred Celluloid

274.

Semantic soul food
Don't eat my people or
Get caught in my teeth

275.

Dark crystal ball world
Buried in a black hole
Liquid ghosts swim free

276.

Shakespeare points to the
Sunflower rarer than a star
My Delirium

277.

When this 6th sense curse
Is lifted adjust to the
Eternal brain face

278.

Special teams football
Won and lost everything
Caught an on-side kick

279.

Grandpa taught me chess
Played Russians in Alaska
During World War 2

280.

Cutting asemic
Science fiction pages with
Calligraphic lines

281.

Tribal scribal tool
Target shooting arrow pens
Range unlimited

282.

Dust everywhere
Learned to write and forgot
My clean ideas

283.

I'm being me if
You don't like it you can read
Something Else Press k

284.

9-inch nail brain spike
Cognition crucifixion
Lunar *Noology*

285.

They call me a slave
Not the child Crusaders
Video game trade

286.

Death died today a
Funeral not attended
No one buried him

287.

Writing origin
Animal tracks in the mud
Fossil feet symbols

288.

Sharpen your eyes to
Hunt & gather Internet
Information lies

289.

Tech burnout leave and
Disconnect me on blank beaches
Meditation wish

290.

Don't fit in today
Except among bar poets
And holy nature

291.

Glowing planet THAT
Cyberspace sanctuary
Robot curator

292.

I'm black and white in
My hardened soul night and day
Does severed sky sleep

293.

Cubed avatar skull
Brain dead bad karma done
Punished 15 years

294.

Wind thoughts blowing through
Lighting up spinal cord trees
X-Mas stoic pain

295.

A brand-new career
Drinking beer to stay sober
Anonymously

296.

Half devil angel
I have bad good thoughts so what
Everyone listens

297.

They click in my head
When they don't like what I think
Nothing is better

298.

Returning guitar
To the sonic atmosphere
Gone solo this time

299.

The voices are late
I am north of a good death
Find me everywhere

300.

Ringing out neurons
Clear interstellar travel
Return home from space

301.

A dead one waiting
Van him milk his fat udder
Force feed him the world

302.

Zyprexa washed down
With mead, beer, and Sertraline
God's sinner cocktail

303.

Clinic for treatment
Fugazi waiting room noose
Psychiatric punk

304.

Slipstream panic block
Escape to other word worlds
Carve the pencils sharp

305.

Disinfecting bleach
Mixes with propaganda
Inane solution

306.

Hot dog blinker juice
Picnic flies on the table
Daughter's first summer

307.

Dad's MG Midget
Lost in the garage mess since
1976

308.

Painter's pants and knife
Scraping paint for a living
Insect bites lead chips

309.

Orange road night lights
Bicycle street takeover
Of swift starless lanes

310.

Missed killing a friend
Throwing a pool cue spear @
Confused hiding eyes

311.

More abuse for the
Divine Internet comedy
Save me Beatrice

312.

Believe in the Sun
Or the Moon pulls you apart
Split hot and cold rocks

313.

Sweatlodge or Sauna
I need out of my pimpled skin
Been inside too long

314.

Live the nothing life
Go nowhere with the shocked world
Buy nothing live down

315.

Congratulations
On your PHD this day
Full debt slavery

316.

Desolate slate state
Late isotope isolate
Chemical conscience

317.

Testosterone tone
Army of the Soul Asylum
Hot cold war still sucks

318.

Ark of Africa
Digitized parchment books
Saint John's Timbuktu

319.

Negative Aids test
Get checked out for peace of mind
What is a condom

320.

Low scars on digits
Spin dried textual weapons
Home and guardian

321.

Popcorn ceiling stones
They throw at you from heaven
Bonded like the sky

322.

Wait for the tumor
To say its last godly words
Snipped off with scissors

323.

New Year's resolutions
Stop being an asshole and
Conquer misery

324.

You win my art quit
Mutilated canvas show
I was born to stop

325.

Poetic jerky
Snafu gelatinous monk
Chili-pepper prayer

326

Sex IT confessions
Running out of humanoids
Don't breed hell babies

327.

The winter solstice
Snow quiets the outside noise
For millions of years

328.

Box of Fish Eye wine
A drink for crazy Zhang Xu
Ink for Huiasu

329.

Religious freedom
God's lingering manifesto
Why hate pan-beliefs

330.

I'm not real says the
Silicon based life form laughing
At my biology

331.

Organ pipe cactus
Camping out in desert mist
South of hot Buckeye

332.

Crying in a beer
Full of my mental garbage
Life gone to fluids

333.

Young witches chanting
Howling razer dark light caul
Sexual capture

334.

Drifting pallid clouds
Grey concrete street magus
Finds a red balloon

335.

Hylton castle cauld
Cold ruins as it should be
Ghost haunts ancestor

336.

Rub ones and zeros
Together to keep warm
Sparky up the fire

337.

A bookstore beer hall
Is my private Valhalla
Priceless poetry

338.

Cold rain and warm snow
Smoke signals the running wind
South Dakota plains

339.

I may be the dead
But I'm not a fossil fuel
Harvest your own death

340.

Graveyard DNA
Dig em all up and explain
With metal shovels

341.

Dying and losing
Virgin mental equations
Tossing calculi

342.

Edible searching
Outdoor freedom foraging
Weeds won't eat themselves

343.

Removable fangs
Cheap red plastic devil horns
Scare them back to church

344.

Light up a peace pipe
In Afghanistan it's time to
End the longest war

345.

Heater broken trip
Snowboarding highest blunt hill
Cold quiet decent

346.

Barefoot summer sand
Walking on alcohol waves
Sunset perfected

347.

Festival chair schism
Cabriolet speed racing
Renaissance Heather

348.

Disaster cuisine
Kitchen bullet unloaded
Cartouche recipe

349.

Chorus voices sing
My stupid belief in God
Post holocaustic

350.

Reinforcement
Ugly sex vs. lab grown
Tissues and issues

351.

My nonsense theory
Voynich Manuscript author
Annius di Viterbo

352.

Laser a quasar
Then tell me how to live long
In a space art hoax

353.

Jam information
Into my tired finite head
Sloshing data soup

354.

Bad news cockabooze
You roaches are surrounded
Scurry from the light

355.

Bling haggle mop head
Raggedy sound disciple
Bass shakes the windows

356.

Blast Pow Kaboom
Shazzap Kerthunk Blammo Zot
Boom Kapow Shazoop

357.

Paved Anthropocene
Calling extinction species
Assaulted graveyard

358.

Murmurs go away
Too easily offended
Happy nothing day

359.

Kick on frequency
Emcee wrapper wisdom punch
Cassette of blind truth

360.

Fish and lobster feast
Snorkel Caribbean coral
Salt leaking goggles

361.

Pizza night headshot
Stupid drunk church brawl
Blood eye revenge fist

362.

Frothing arms dealers
Celebrate my 9/11
Birth with war wishes

363.

If I fight it will
Be for social democracy
Not the privileged

364.

Smoking a pipe near
The cool fire with gas station
Microwave burgers

365.

Eagle's peak lookout
Taylors falls bowling cauldron
Franconia twist

366.

Mainstream Jesus ears
Break the concentration camps
Sadist separations

367.

We should make heaven
Happen but we don't live long
Cackling money gloats

368.

Idiot crossing
Slow down and enjoy passing
Through pearly chomp gates

369.

Twisted illiterate
Learns linguistic gymnastics
Vocal vocation

370.

First fortunate cookie
Premonition for success
Ability crazy

371.

Mexico highway
Milky Way sky overhead
Dark bouncing truck bed

372.

You have beaten out
All the fucks I have given
Suck the liquid store

373.

They call THAT stupid
Null contributing critics
Of my cyber world

374.

I was circumcised
Chopped off on my birthday
Don't pass the custom

375.

Nuclear family
TV static in the fallout
Canned green bean hotdish

376.

Raised as Lutheran
With a Hebrew Viking name
Agnostic theist

377.

Solar system trap
Naked together time warp
Star glowing engines

378.

Driving fast go-carts
Wisconsin death's vacation
Pete's locked hotel door

379.

I've got the look
Young Santa or old Jesus
Ho Ho Anarchrist

380.

Once an Atheist
Religion oscillation
Now I pray for rain

381.

Ocean acidifies
I hate the rude planet death
As I type on plastic

382.

Cold Gitchi-Gami
Agate shore lighthouse shipwrecks
I've been baptized twice

383.

Crash course living needs
Take care of elders and children
Change diapers robots

384.

In Chicago blues
Slept in Tina's Toyota
Blanket cold car lot

385.

Alternator died
Ten miles outside Sioux Falls
Armed mechanic helps

386.

7734
Exercise in memory
Snide calculations

387.

He pulled up his shirt
To show me the bullet wounds
In cabinet class

388.

A kiss on the cheek
Shots in drunken poverty
Today's fantasy

389.

Will they clone my ass
If I run for astronaut of
The book business

390.

Won too three for five
Sicks seven ate nine ten e
Leven twelve thirteen

391.

Born '73
Fender Ford Mustang
Pure car and guitar

392.

Carbon sequester
To get where I need to go
I walk, bus, or bike

393.

Give me classic words
First mumbled after Tao lakes
Of cool consciousness

394.

The world's best dad thought
Some parents go through wild hell
For long freedom hair

395.

Underground film maker
Making my avant-horror
Divinity debut

396.

The eternal well
Of life in a connected room
Wifi needle eye

397.

Teleportation
Boomerang my stick and dirt
Collection of time

398.

Cheap toe hurting shoes
Itching polyester pants
Mom taught Sunday school

399.

Paranoid nightmare
Peripheral vision poem
Explains the world well

400.

Leukemia pulse
Sanguine scar on God's lost heart
Disease full of loss

401.

Coen bros dinning
Kids Jolly Troll smorgasbord
Animatronics

402.

My short movie poems
Cinematic gif epics
Cult director's cut

403.

Genetic memory
Connected and wind dispersed
Diaspora seeds

404.

The souls of raindrops
Small and powerful when lashing
Vaulted tears sans salt

405.

Offer tobacco
Thunder Nation Pow Wow drum
Finndian to the end

406.

Forgive me Goddess
A rich guy with no money
Out book collecting

407.

I want true lessons
In how to make stone tools and
Super computers

408.

Enjoy this full life
Have sex and eat fine cuisine
Cope with good beer friends

409.

Now that you have read
My life story Hei Kuu poems
Where to next Earth stars

Micheal Jacobson/MK JCBSN selfie portrait.

Michael Jacobson is a writer, artist, and independent curator from Minneapolis, Minnesota USA. His books include **The Giant's Fence** (Ubu Editions), **Action Figures** (Avance Publishing), **Mynd Eraser** (YouTube), **The Paranoia Machine**, and his latest collected writings **Works & Interviews** (Post-Asemic Press); he is also co-editor of **An Anthology Of Asemic Handwriting** (Punctum Books). Besides writing books, he curates a gallery for asemic writing called **The New Post-Literate**, and he sits on the editorial board of **SCRIPTjr.nl**. Recently, he was published in **The Last Vispo Anthology** (Fantagraphics), and he curated the Minnesota Center for Book Arts exhibit: **Asemic Writing: Offline & In The Gallery**. His online interviews include **Full of Crow**, **SampleKanon**, **Asymptote Journal**, **Twenty Four Hours**, **David Alan Binder**, and at **Medium**. In the past he created the cover art for **Rain Taxi**'s 2014 winter issue. Since 2017, he has published books of experimental and asemic writing on his imprint **Post-Asemic Press**. He also founded and administers the **asemic writing Facebook group**. In his spare time, he is working on designing a cyberspace planet dubbed **THAT**. His Ello studio can be found here: **@asemicwriter**.

www.ingramcontent.com/pod-product-compliance
Lightning Source LLC
Chambersburg PA
CBHW071720040426
42446CB00011B/2146